CLARE SHAW

Flood

BLOODAXE BOOKS

ISBN: 978 1 78037 420 8

First published 2018 by
Bloodaxe Books Ltd,
Eastburn,
South Park,
Hexham,
Northumberland NE46 1BS.

www.bloodaxebooks.com
For further information about Bloodaxe titles
please visit our website or write to
the above address for a catalogue.

Supported using public funding by
**ARTS COUNCIL
ENGLAND**

Cover design: Neil Astley & Pamela Robertson-Pearce.

Printed in Great Britain by Bell & Bain Limited, Glasgow, Scotland, on
acid-free paper sourced from mills with FSC chain of custody certification.

For my people

ACKNOWLEDGEMENTS

Acknowledgements are due to the editors of *The Moth*, where some of these poems first appeared.

'Rainhill Psychiatric Hospital 1992', 'This is a man', 'For the love of' and 'Just look' were first published in *Tom Woods: the DPA Work – Photographs of Rainhill Hospital and Camel Laird Shipyard* by Cian Quayle, Audrey Linkman, Clare Shaw and Tom Woods (Stiedl, 2018).

'My father was no ordinary man' and 'My mother was a verified miracle' were first published in *Project Boast: poems by 28 women*, edited by Rachel Bentham and Alyson Hallett (Triarchy Press, 2018).

Thanks are due to the University of Huddersfield and the Royal Literary Fund for the support and the opportunities provided to me during my time as a Royal Literary Fellow. Special thanks to Kim Moore, John Foggin and Keith Hutson for their advice, support and encouragement.

With love to Niamh, Jamima and Hebden Bridge.

CONTENTS

What do I know

I know I am not registered to the correct address.
I know cigarettes are bad for me,
I should drink more water.
I know unstable rocks can ruin your day
and screes are a quick way down.

I know you should carry a map and a torch.
I know how to use a compass.
I know there is no definitive proof
of the biological basis of mental illness.
I know how to climb. I can drink from a stream.
I know what it feels like to drown
and not to remember my name.

I know you are angry with me and I don't know why.
I know most of what I need to know
can be found on Google. *When a girl is angry with you
it means she is attracted to you.* I know
this is not correct. I know how to count to three
in five different languages
including sheep. *Yan Tan Tethera.* See.

I know that I have taken the wrong path.
I know clear, cold and natural is not enough.
I know dead sheep can kill.
There are invisible micro-organisms in the water by millions –
ciarda microsporidia protozoa flagellate ciliata
cryptosporidium – and I know them by name.

I know that acting as though you know what you are doing
as almost as good as knowing
but this is not true on a mountain.
I know the telephone number to my first home
I know it is all my fault but I can't stop it.

I know that sadness tastes of smoke.
I know my father tasted of smoke.
I know how stars are made because I made one
and it was a simple matter of asking.
I know sometimes I just have to ask,
the rock will tell me which way to move
and sometimes I do not fall.

I know I have made you mad.
I know it is time for bed.
I know we are mostly made of stars.
I know there are 10^{22} stars in the universe
but I don't know how many that it is.

Who knows what it's like

to grow up outnumbered,
to be one in a hundred –

to talk the wrong talk, to walk the wrong path,
to be laughed at and spat at,
to get used to that stuff?
To live the wrong life; to be from the wrong town?
To not have the sense or the chance

to fit in, to keep your head down –
to dance the wrong dance
with the wrong kind of man?
To dance the wrong dance
with a girl?

My god, it took guts
on those very cold nights
in those very small boats.
Each week I climbed Pendle in not-the-right-boots,
walked my heels raw in no coat –

but they'd hung all the witches
and buried the Nutters
so it was back to the pictures
and maps of old places
looking for names I might know. Oh

Todmorden – valley of honey and sun!
Hebden – oh promised land!

Over the moor's broad shoulder; down
over its muscular arm –
it was way more than home knit
and joss stick and dope.
More than moorland and ruined farm.

It was climbers and folkies and vegans and hippies
and commies and junkies and straight-talking farmers
and anarchist punks and hikers and drunks
and peaceniks and loonies of various colours
and lesbian mothers and day-tripping shoppers

and artists and dreamers and rain blowing sideways
on communal houses in minus-ten winters
and poets and sun on the stone.
I grew up outnumbered, one hundred to one.
I found my own people. My kin.

Instructions for coping in terrible times

Learn to swim. If you have time,
secure your home
before the expected rain.

Pay attention. Floods can happen
in minutes. Turn off utilities
at the main switches.

Avoid any movement
that causes pain.
When a warning is issued – leave.

Control the bleeding.
If you are taking cover in a church hall,
padlock your bags against theft.

Always listen to the instructions
authorities give you. Do not be alone.
Identify where you can go –

a friend in another town,
a motel, for example.
Keep your gas tank full.

Cover the burn with dry, clean dressings.
Don't drive through moving currents
on the way.

If your car stalls in rising waters,
abandon it immediately. Accept small favours.
Seize every opportunity to stay dry.

Take what is brought by the river
in your stride. Eat meat if you have to.
Do not fall. The weather will change

and all damage is relative.
If you notice an unfamiliar smell,
have it inspected. Write it all down.

Be prepared to quit at a moment's notice.
Accept what you are entitled to.
Do not drown.

For the journey

For snow on the fields for months.
For gloves and the heater. For heat and my daughter,
the passenger seat. For winter stayed late,
the small lane made lethal with ice.

For the lane, for a year's worth of rain,
for the river, the anger of water, the threat –
more rain yet – of flooding, for overworked gutters
outspilling, the quick lakes spreading

like grief. For every day grief. For the flight
of the once-glimpsed kingfisher flying,
for his blue, for the air growing purple with morning.
For every small thing that can fly

and for those who will never. For me
choked with sleep and not-enough-sleep,
with nightmares and letters. With what came
straight at us. For fury the height of a hill,

as cold as the weather, as strong as a brother.
The roar of the engine, the rhythm of wiper,
the owl and the blue trees' shudder and whisper.
For the forest that did not care

for my daughter. For all of my prayers.
For the comfort of shoes
and the Co-op and shops in their regular rows,
for all things familiar and worn. For the everyday

pattern of lane, road and rain.
For the lollipop man. For all the lights on.
For the life that came crashing down.
For how things carry on. For her face like the sun.

Late Afternoon, Allan Bank

Hello. Rain makes the world shy.
It is where
evening happens, and being alone.

I'm not interested in squirrels,
only the gutters
and the stories they tell:

the sadness of wet wood
and the world
seen flat through a window,

only the little birds which
rain cannot stop
or silence, and this desk:

its pens, magnifying glass, typewriter,
messages left behind:
Today is a loveley day

Under the trees, darkness gathers.
Today is over
alen bank I have come

before it hardly began.
to do somepainting.
It's a long drive home

I love you and so much
is broken. *I*
don't know how to begin

Through the lens, my words
are all forest
but my pen, my pen

knows the way.

Water as Religion

Born into it. From the outset,
it was the element you swam in.
You learnt to accept it

or drown.
Fish are given no choice,
and you weren't either.

You saw people wrecked there.
There was bread
but not much to breathe.

As you went deeper,
the pressure increased.
The effect on the body

was terrible.
It could cover up anything
and not show a ripple.

Standing up to it was
impossible –
there was always the threat

of storm.
But sometimes, you still drift
in a hymn

and you are home
and will come to no harm.
Your faith will keep you

afloat.
You are more than half
made of it.

More than half of you aches
to return.

And still I don't know

I still don't know what it was
that woke us, suddenly,
both as one. It wasn't the chimes,

it wasn't the neighbours,
it wasn't the lights switched on.
Maybe the room was too cold, I was shaking

and I think I could see you
breathing, silver.
though it was late summer

and we hadn't worn coats all week.
The lamps went out one-by-one
and now the road was a river of darkness

and there was a thrill
like disaster impending –
something bigger than joy or pain.

And both like that
in our T-shirts and shorts
the cotton still warm from sleep,

we walked down the path to the beach
where the sea was sighing
and pounding and crashing

and the boats were rocking.
Your eyes were creatures,
your fingers were darkness

and the sea was all of our past
and future
and way, way out, there were lights on the water.

We hadn't touched all night
but your hand was in mine
and your hair smelled clean

and your skin, your skin
was a dream.

Lovehearts

True Lips

So all I remember
is night
and how your room was a river;

how I couldn't breathe
or see straight
and how it was more like drowning than swimming,

how your face was an open gate:
it answered all of my questions,
how definite was your kiss

– your kiss was the sentence
I wanted to speak.
Your kiss was a tall man, standing up

and you walked like
none of the doors were shut.
You walked like there was a path, well-lit

and you just walked right in.

I will

Because I was drunk and you were bright;
because my head was a dance.

Because I was scared and my blood was storm –
force ten – the windows all blown in,
because you were clean and brown and slim.
Because your kiss was a coin;

was sharp, precise; was loose change, silver
and then another, then another
and the air was a fast road speeding past
and there was no going back.

Because I followed you into the dark
and I was all abroad.
A small boat, rocked;
my moorings slipped

and your hands were ships and the night was black
and the wind was loud and there were no birds
because I followed you up the stairs.
I have never seen such stars.

New Love

is shiny with hope. It opens the chest
like cold air. The ribs creak, unaccustomed –
then love pours out, a jackpot,
as yellow and bright as fruit.

New love is a ride, headfirst, steep.
Trees are a blur; air is water and roar –
the heart rests up for the upwards slope.
For the moment the slog resumes.

New love is a joke, a trick. Not magic –
but you still can't help being amazed. *How do you do that?*
Upbeat, it is always new music,
even the same old tunes.

It starts out small, unbearably weak,
constantly hungry, wide-beaked.
You know you should leave it
but hopeful-at-heart, you still try

tweezering worms down its throat
through the night.
The odds are dead-set against it, but
sleep-starved, you watch it

survive.
It grows fatter and strong.
Then you recognise those feathers.
And you know – very deeply – that song.

Double

In praise of shoes, and the feet within them
In awe of those who go without them.

In praise of the ankle and its tough construction.
In praise of breasts and the hands to touch them.

Praise for the ovary in the booming dark.
In praise of how animals boarded the ark.

In praise of wings and in praise of lips
sipping extra-strong coffee from tiny cups:

with thanks for what makes the head spin –
whisky and gin, packing it in

and all that comes in double measures.
Praise all things that come together –

salt and pepper, sun and moon.
Praise to the couplet and praise to the twin.

Thanks for the duet and the almost-rhyme
of the double bed in the double room.

For the quick blue fish of your quick blue eyes
and for both your brain's hemispheres. Praise to your thighs.

Hydrology

An energy brings us together –
but at some point
we will change.

Of course
the sun has everything to do with it
and laws we don't understand

but we know it is inevitable
and there is no music in it.
Water must change its state

and everything is about water:
how it forms; how it rises and falls
and the rain and the clouds

are relentless.
We accept this
though the process is not without pain.

All that it takes is heat:
at some point,
we come apart.

It ends, it begins
with the rain.

Weather warning

The weather's all wrong
and nothing can right it. Wherever I am,
there's a sound in the background
like threat. The wind knows
all of my secrets.
It hates that it cannot speak.

All night, it rages. The garden is battered,
the small path is lost to mud.
Slates have slipped. There's damp in the bricks
and the floors are dirty.
No matter how high the heating,
I cannot get warm.

When I sleep, I dream in yellow;
sun pouring down me
like rain. Then I'm naked
and everything I touch is hot.
Sky glares; flowers are open.
Bushes are loaded with fruit. I'm a shit.

Morning. You're on the bed's far side.
The room smells of something hidden.
The river is angry with rain.
Roads are blocked and the lines are down.
I stretch out my arm
but can't reach you. I cannot reach you at all.

How I heard

I heard rain like conversation,
I heard the warning, more to come.
I heard the front door slamming

and I heard my phone insisting.
I heard Todmorden was going,
Mytholmroyd had gone.

I did not hear the siren.
I heard a sound like anger
and all night long, the river.

I heard rumours of disaster.
Like pain, I heard the water
and I heard the school was under

and I could not get warm.
I saw the blue lights flashing
and I heard my neighbours shouting.

I heard warning, I heard warning –
yes I saw the river rising
but I did not see this coming

Roads and paths covered; flash flooding on steeper slopes

The air is forest.
The road is blocked with trees.
There is noise between them
and no word except *river*;
the canal is fast river; the path
is deep river; the river is a story
that can't be believed.

The birds have all left the woods.
The lane is a ripped-up book.
And as much as you know of rain –
this rain is taking everything.
Your clothes forget themselves,
your shoes have never been dry.

It has drowned the rabbits.
They could not escape
from the cage where you kept them.
It is lifting the hens in their coop –
you can still hear them scream.
It breaks your phone

and the lights.
You are left in the total dark.

When your town is a river
and everywhere you love
is going under;
when even the boats can't float
and the water is at your door and rising,
when the mice have all fled upstairs;

when no one can reach you,
the only choice you can make
is what you can lift and save,
is not to forget you can leave –

is to wade with the weight of a child on your shoulders,
to follow instructions for crossing deep water
though the current grows steadily stronger and deeper.

Your house is a river.
Now swim.

Flood Town

I am the track
blocked with rubble. I am rubble.
I am the teatime commuter
come home to a town in disaster. I am on my phone.
I am the man saying *fuck*
over and over.
I am up to my axles in muck.

I am that one car floating.
I am those who did not make it
up the hill.
I am the battery, dead in the cold.
I am the phone's blank screen.

I am the siren that sounded too late.
I am the neighbour with the cigarette.
I am too wet to smoke.
I am the gate you leaned on.
I am the schools, all shut.

I am the children. I don't know whether
to cry. *Where should I go?*
I am the mother, knee deep.
I cannot stop saying *Fuck*.
I would like to go home now. I am the rain.
A town in ruins. Fuck.
Fuck.

Why did the sand blush?

His touch.

Why did the sun rise?
Her eyes.

Why did the birds sing?
So young.

Why did the sun burn?
She'd learn.

Why did the star fish?
All hush.

Why did the fish net?
Tight-caught.

Why did the ship wreck?
Her neck.

And did the rainbow?
No. No.

Why did the sea shell?
Don't tell.

Why did the sun set?
Forget.

Why did the moonlight?
Each night.

Why did the sea weep?
No sleep.

Grabbed

Start with the lake, the cold blue
slap of it;
now pan to an empty sky.

A girl on a bike,
downhill. Catch the river
of breeze on her face.

Track to a churchyard – flowers,
tall weeds; show
how the shade turns suddenly dark.

Move, quick –
to a moment of capture.
Grabbed, she is sack,

she is hauled and helpless.
His arms are strong water
in flood.

Freeze-frame:
on her back
and those strange instructions;

the malice of ground
baked hard. Before her,
a blankness of wall.

The sky must be empty
of God, oh God,
she feels nothing at all

no touch like murder,
no grizzle of scalp
on her thighs,

no fingers like fire, no
body that blocks out the light.
Make her not die.

And when it is over
zoom in.
To the small hands sweating like meat

and the flowers that she gripped
throughout. Crushed.
Make us feel it:

the shame
of the burning air, god
make her not care.

Rainhill Psychiatric Hospital 1992

It felt like this – a process of loss
and nothing replaced.
Sky, seen from a darkened room.

How the years were a lot like water:
how they passed me by,
how they dragged me under,

how they carried me to distant lands
where I could not speak
my own tongue.

I left the whole world behind.
When I put out my hand,
the ground wasn't there

and there was no shore
or far lights shining,
just the strange things the ocean brought us –

mainly lighters and broken glass.
Out of my element, I learnt to swim
and was never alone.

We were legion and came from the stars.
It hurt us to fall
so far. Where are we?

Can you point out this place on a map?
Though some of us will not talk
we are not without voices. Listen.

Nobody intended this story
but I have written it down
on my arms.

And now you can read it:
life
was a land I remember far off.

Then it crumbled beneath
my feet.

This is a man

This is dust. This is Merry Christmas.
These are all my own teeth.
This is the only home I have lived in.
This is the empty cup.

This is my baccy, my tin.
These are my matches, I bought them.
This is lino, cracked. These are stains.
I cannot be sure what made them.

This is a message I was given.
This is my name. This is very alone.
This is the way I have always stood.
This is a terrible man.

This is the jumper that does not fit.
This is my cap, my cigarette.
This is the site of the Friday night social.
This is my favourite song.

This is the door and no one using it.
This is eight miles from town.
This is a study in shadow and light.
This is the wrong way out.

This is my shirt and my trousers too short.
This is an afternoon I cannot see the end of.
This is punishment. This is where I was sent.
This is no formal composition.

This is the chair. This is not my pen.
This is a man.
The only home I have ever known.
This is the curtain. This is the bin.

For the love of

For his lovely smell of soap and man,
his wife's soft hands,
his collar, put just neat, just-right;

his lovely pills all-sleep, no-thought.
His make-it-straight, his clever-speak,
for his desk and all his tightness.

For his lines and his right-way-upness.
For his bright-shine shoes all fit, just-nice.
For the work all written through him.

For his silence, deep as wood.
Not interested.
His make-it-good, his far-as-God,

his pass-like-cloud, like judgement, God –
for the future swims in his blood like silver,
the children who swim in his blood.

For lights in lamps and smell of home.
For fires on full and floors washed clean,
for tea in mugs and my own room.

For the walls that bloom
where he walks.

For his quiet, firm no-scream,
no-shout. No kick, no slap. No finger-poke.
No hands that burn like star.

For his crossing road, his driving car,
his straight-as-line, his strong his clean,
his rock to lean on, solid-safe,

his freshmint breath,
for the words that fall from him like stone.
For straw in drowning hands.

His hard-as-brick, his lightning strike,
his knowing-what, his bright white shock
his wipe-it-out, his make-it-stop

for the love of God
for sleep

Just look

The shelves tell you half of my story.
They are empty of anything good.

That tin of sweets
with no sweets in it;

if you want me to talk,
just look

to the books
which nobody reads;

to the chess board
with none of its pieces.

Don't ask me to say how I feel;
ask the carpet.

It is like
it has never been clean.

I don't need to speak out.
It's clear at first sight

that the table is angles
and does not count

and the chairs
are as red as sin

and none of the white
has ever been white

and nothing about this has ever been right
and the plant does not fit its pot.

Yes.
That's it.

And the corridor flooded with light.

Grim

'But I feel very sorry for the poor children, all the same.'

THE WOODCUTTER

No light in that darkness
to lead them or save them.
No one to hear them and nothing to guide them.

Too young to be out there alone
and so hungry.
The forest at night is so terribly rowdy;

one shriek is too much like another.
Owl is rabbit is fox-scream is murder
is brother and sister.

The wind in the branches is whisper and water.
The moon is a ghost.
Path is trap. Black.

They should not have been there alone –
in that house in the clearing; its lacework of icing;
the sugary blaze of the sweets.

So young and so hungry. So terribly pretty.
All that colour and candy – who would have believed it?
Who didn't suspect it,

who hadn't yet guessed it – did fuck all about it –
his jacket of gold and his skin thick as leather,
his burgundy chair like a throne?

They should not have been there alone.
Who's to blame –
for the way that it feels when you're fifteen and under

you're led to the forest and sold down the river
and he's old as the hills, as your mother, your father
and all these years later

they're telling the same story over and over and
(there's millions watching his hands up your jumper)
over and over and over and over?

Who said

Who said about the boy and girl?
Who told that tale?

Who said they were alone
and lost – I lured them in –
who cast that stone?
Who said the boy was small and thin?

Who licked my panes? Who bit my bricks?
Could you pick them out
from a group of six?
Who stuffed themselves till they were sick?
Who told you I was there?

Who said the girl was tall and fair?
Who stole my fruit? Who ate my bread?
Who said I tucked them up in bed?
Who said I touched her hair?
Who asked me why? Who told that lie –
the birds that sang in the summer's sky?
the wolves that howled at the moon?

Did they tell you that my house was clean
and all my own? Who wrecked my roof?
Who told the truth?
Who smelt the honey on my breath?
Who wrecked my house? Who plucked my rose?
Who tore my clothes?
Who opened up the oven door? Who left me there?

I caught my fish, I earned my crust
I broke the ice, I killed the beast.
I trapped and shot, I dug the land,
I built it all by hand and sweat.
Who saw my dreams? Who read my mind?
Who knew the secrets that I kept?
Who said I watched them as they slept?

Who told about the boy and girl?
Who tells my tale?
Who said I was? Who said I did?
Who said I wasn't chopping wood?
Who sang like a little bird?
Who wrote these words?

Telling Tales

I was in the forest. They said
if I was older they would marry me,
when I got older I would be their wife.
They took my sisters for drinks.
We got drunk with them. We were children,
we were sent to the forest alone.

I was in a station. The policewoman said
if you weren't so pretty
it wouldn't keep happening. My mother laughed
but at least I was pretty,
I was left in a forest. The woodcutter was there
and the witch, I was all chopped up.

The birds were singing, they said
some little girls tell lies. This is no lie:
the toilets in the station were made of steel
and so were the walls. They echoed if anyone
moved. I stayed very still.
If I am quiet now I can remember it;

the last time I was whole.
I was lost in the forest, no brother was with me
and the witches had eaten my sisters,
my sisters were witches. I will not enter
the toilets; they are only for Ladies
and I left my lady behind. I put on this shirt.

I will chop the woods down on my own;
I will burn them. There will be no trees.
No animals, nowhere to hide. Just fire.

Nothing I'm afraid to write except for words

Maybe all that there is
are these broken pots
and the moon on a concrete yard

in the dark.
Maybe I was born to the dark.
Maybe my name is a lie

and the moon is not bright
and those hills I once walked
were a dream.

Maybe there was no snow
and no singing,
no winter sun rising, maybe

I just stayed at home:
there was no other path
and I couldn't build it.

You were right, you were right, I'll regret
what I did. Maybe I did it
because I was weak, I was mad,

maybe the moon is all in my head
and no one believes me,
why should they?

You were right. I wouldn't know
the truth if it bit me.
Just look at me –

here are the scars.

My father was no ordinary man

My father could fly. He needed no father –
he had mother, the hunger of four older brothers –
my father was one of an army of brothers
and he learnt all the ways of men.

My father was handsome and worshipped by women.
His loins were a river: they flowed with his children
and he was the fountain of truth we all drank from
and when he held forth we would not interrupt him.
My father named every flower in the garden,
each star in the night by the right constellation.
He knew all the birds by their song

and they sang it. My father could never be wrong.
His hands were a gun and they brought down the rabbit.
He fed us on flesh that was studded with bullets.
There was fire in his fist, there was gold in his pocket.
My father turned water to wine and he drank it –
he needed no prayer and no God

for he was the word and he rang like a hammer.
Oh, my father was victor; he rode on our shoulders,
he rode deep inside us. We carried my father
through hell and high water,
we proved ourselves worthy of love

and his love was a river in flood.
The sun made him happy.
The truth was soft mud in his hands, oh truly
he was the truth and he was the glory.
He filled all the rooms with his song and his story,
his whisper could silence a house

for my father bore pain that you could not imagine.
His forearms were scarred and his fingers were broken.
His lungs were a pit and his heart was a puncture.

47

Oh, my father was hard and my father was tender
and his hand was a mark
we will all wear forever.

My mother was a verified miracle

My mother was church door where millions entered.
My mother was tower where four kestrels roosted –
my mother was hooded, she plunged and she hovered.
She flew at the speed of the wind, oh
my mother had wings and her voice was an organ,
she was seraph and cherub and throne and dominion.
My mother was bright with flame.

My mother was saint and my mother was martyr
and she was the light floating over the water.
My mother was whale and I rode safe inside her –
I was blessed and I came out clean
for my mother was sermon and she was the mountain
and she was the tree and the nails and the Roman
and her rafters were oak and her stone was all golden.

My mother said Let there be light
and she was the light. My mother was fruit
and we peopled the earth in her name
for my mother was sun and my mother was thunder.
My mother would get at the truth if it killed her –
she laid waste to the nations for me did my mother
and I could not run from her love

for my mother was choir, she was every bird singing
and she was the song and will not be forgotten.
My mother was angel, my mother was fallen.
She suffered the children and fed them on nothing.
My mother was bread
and my mother was broken
and she was the ark. She was darkness. The ocean.

Low lying regions inundated. Large objects begin to float

My man was not blameless but he knew his own mind.
He loved his sons, his God, his goats.
We were solid as wood, as steady as bread.
It was not perfect: it was what I had.
I brought up boys in a time of war.
I loved them. I had no choice.

And this is my voice:
you would not believe the violence;
how the ground was covered in minutes;
how quickly our valley was Nile.

When the river came with a sound like battle
and when all the waters were one
then we knew how angry we'd made him
and it was too late to run.
When I tell you I feared for my life

for my children – you cannot imagine.
When I say, I saw people drown,
they looked in my face and I could not help them –
ours was the only boat on that ocean;
a boat the size of a zoo, a mansion;
a sea the size of the world.

I lived to see what I loved destroyed
and all my world was unmade.

Forty days. The boredom and stink
and the darkness. No wonder
the birds pulled out their feathers
and the bear banged his head on the wall.
And when the rain stopped,
then the silence.

The mountains a dream in the waters beneath us.
I think, that day, there was sun.

When floods recede,
they don't leave a world made shiny
and bright. For years, I'll be cleaning up shit.
No bird nor branch can make this right.
No trick of the light. No I'll-never-do-it
again. No god or man.

I loved him. I had no choice.
And this is my voice:
it takes more than a dove
and I will not forgive.

Divorce

When you are in deep water,
you will have to get out of it –
quick.

If your car has submerged,
fight panic.
Switch on the inside light –

the headlights too (if they work).
Help rescuers see
where you are.

If the windows are jammed,
try to break them. Kick hard.
It is best to not to leave

through the door.
If you ever knew where the engine was,
recall it now.

The car won't go down straight away.
You must use every moment
to get out. Push children out first.

Don't save anything but lives.
If you are unable to open a window,
keep your head.

You may still have a chance to survive.
When the inside is filling
with water

there should be a minute of air.
Prepare.
When the car is nearly full,

take a deep breath.
Push open a door with your feet.
If you try too soon,

the pressure will beat you
(to be honest,
the odds are already slim).

Rescue effort

Look.

It has stopped.
You lifted your sofa on blocks.
You saved some stock.
You did whatever you could.

You worked hard.
Your daughter was never afraid.

Now look.
The sun has come back,
hedges are heavy with light.
Fields shine

and though sheep are still waiting
for rescue,
they will be saved.
As will you.

Measures of Goodness

Those swilling for others.
Those who form armies of buckets and brushes;
those bailing water from fast-filling cellars.
Those making cuppas for neighbours and strangers:
those who would see no one cold.

Those saving homes
when their own have gone under.
Those stood behind or in front of the cameras –
who do it for nothing or glory or wages.
Those posting pictures on Facebook and Twitter.

Those sending texts; those risking their necks;
those stopping their cars for a look.

Those who battle to cattle and horses;
who shoulder the weight of the sheep,
their soaked fleeces; those wading waist-deep
on deep roads to old ladies.
Those on bridges that will not hold.

Those driving all night to bring fodder to farmers.
Those making profit from badly built houses.

Those who make thunder;
those born to power,
who shoulder the blame
for the rain and the river.
Those who have ruined your town;

who have choked up the drains;
who have broken your home.
Those who send water to drown all the chickens.
Those who would watch you go down
(and your children); who are rain.

And those who are sun.

This is for Stanley and Dan

the men in the scrapyard whose skin
is permanently darkened, who are
always busy. This is for the mystery
of their work – they throw tea
on the ground like a blessing –

how they smell – like my car –
of sweet dirt; for their comfort
with money and muck. This is for my suspension
which they mended
though the car fell down on its wheels

and this is for tools, for their singing,
the rich slop of oil
and for sky, reflected. For dogs
who should live here all weathers;
this, for the rattle of chains.

This is for cars: those overwritten
with terrible stories,
those with smashed faces,
those fractured and cracked, those totally fucked.
And for those who return them to life:

how their diet is terrible.
How their teeth are bad.
How their hands are scarred
but nothing dismays them –
those who sort things; who hack them to pieces.

This is for men who are damaged beyond salvage,
This is for Stanley and Dan
who are busted and ruptured,
who are torn up and gutted.
Whose parts are missing, who cannot be mended.

Major structures destroyed; terrain significantly altered

The valley has shifted.
That landscape you took for granted –
whatever it meant

has changed.
Rivers have altered their courses;
centuries-old bridges have failed.

No number of sandbags
could stop this.
You will not walk here again.

Your boots and your compass
were useless.
She has gone. She has left you

mapless.
Now, you must find your own way
in the darkness.

Find your own way
by the stars.

A love song to punctuation

I knew you by touch
and not rules and you held me
and you were the space where I breathed.

Your fingers were rambling sentences;
they wrote all across me.
I was lost in your story.

We laid down like commas,
curled close.
Our chests were no need

for full-stops.
Your breath on my neck
an ellipsis. Your fingers...

We came in multiples, gasping –
a series of dashes
we didn't need closure,

our movements were made
without system and order
and they kept all your housemates awake.

In the dark, the marks of our questions
were glitter and hook.
In bed, you grew very still

and I knew you by ache.
Then we were a book
full of distance and break,

suddenly
in the wrong tense.

When did it happen?
We said what we did not mean
there was no rhythm

no sense of direction
the stress
was in the wrong place

we were quick changing weather
and the words were a river all
fast-flowing water

and there was nothing gentle
or still. Still you ask me now
what is the point?

You are necessary
to my story.
Without you, my arms have no meaning

or structure. You hold me together.
I'm nothing without you
but words.

Catastrophic devastation; damage complete

Enough of rapid water.
Enough of the current and roar.
Enough of the anger. Enough of the Calder.
Enough of the Eden and Lune and the Cocker,
the Aire and the Derwent, the Ribble and Greta.
Enough of the Don and the Dee and the Culter.

Enough of the waiting. Enough of the checking.
Enough of waking up each night to listen
to rain, the rhythm of rain on the roof.
Enough of the grief, of packing your stuff.
Enough of slipping and losing your footing,
of trying to stand up again.

Enough of being wet, of water.
Enough of tap and bath and shower;
enough of gentle rain on flowers.
Enough of love and where it takes us –
ruined places. Enough of broken shops
and homes. Enough of dreams. Enough of plans.

Enough of made-up words for weather.
Enough of words that did not save us.
Enough of friends with shut-down faces.
Enough of toppled trees, uprooted;
enough of major structures shifted,
enough of wood and concrete lifted,

enough of nothing left
to lift, enough of nothing left.
Enough of loss. Enough of luck.
Enough of Whalley, Keswick, York.
Enough of what will not come back.
Enough of what we could not change.

Enough of grief and anger, love –
enough. Enough of rain.

Love is not

Love is not this small room, nor this house,
all of its unpainted surfaces.
Love is not the floor, new with varnish.
It is definitely not

these jeans. Love is not sat
at this table, it is not
nearly midnight.
Love is not this pen, not the tap
and its drip-drip-drip.

Love is not toothache. It
cannot be dulled
with whisky; love is not whisky
or a bottle of any size; it is not the violin
slung on the woodpile, nor the sofa.
It is not the unplugged TV.

Love is not on the shelf. It is not books
or dragonfly; it does not stand
for hope. Love is not hope, nor the box
which reads I ♥ YOU THIS MUCH.
Love does not heart you, not even this much
and it is not this stuff in your mouth.
Love is not the colour of water

falling down hills after rain.
Love is not light, not the door,
not even the wrong one
down to the spidery cellar.
It does not lead onto the street, or upstairs.
When you look outside
love is not the wall, nor the gutter.
It is definitely not the moon.

Pinnacle Ridge

First came the rain.

Then morning,
cooler than we'd expected;
the walk-in much tougher, the climb.
We should have known.
The guide book steered us

to features we could not find.
The climbers –
righteous with rope and harness –
warned us
there was no easy way round.

Below us,
five hundred metres of drop
and fuck all to grip.
No book could make sense
of that slope.

What took us up there?
Nothing was what we expected.
We were utterly unprepared.
What made us persist –
sky, slate?

Desire to impress, to get high
by one means or
the other,
one slip from disaster?
The only comfort you could offer

was the hope we might not die.
But the chances were,
we'd be hurt.
The sky doesn't give a shit.
Rock knows its own way up.

There was truly no way
to retreat.
We were left to our own good luck –
which, like weather and slate
did not hold.

Though we made it
far enough to look back
and be shocked at the risks that we took –
I'm not proud.
But if you would lead,

I'd follow. Knowing this time
what to expect.
To hear strangers calling my name.
To be hurt
in ways I could never predict.

To have blood on my hands.
Then the rain.

The Cruellest Month

On the next table, two women
are talking about *The Archers*.
If a man is found innocent, it means
he's guilty – that's the way the law works
they say. Did you listen
to Shirley Manson this morning?

I don't know anyone who hasn't had this cold
and it's a bad one.
The flowers came through too early this year
but they kept on coming and
though the trees are still leafless,
I've always loved blossom more.

Put me in a room full of redcurrant
and leave me there,
I have no reason to believe this sensation
that something terrible is about to happen.
April is all about renewal
and the mist on the hill is beautiful

but I don't know if I can kiss you again.
There wasn't a part of me you didn't touch
and it might be fever
but when I tell myself
this is a river, over and over,
I don't feel a thing

and though it's spring, fact is,
when it happened,
something inside of me stopped.
Most of the cafés have opened again.
Some will not. Shirley says
we need to talk about trauma

and she should know
and though I'm all for being human
when the river came this December,
it took half of our town.
When I told you I loved you,
I meant it –

but I mean this more:
I will not go south in the winter.
I'm not pinning my hopes
on summer, or spring for that matter,
but the willow is coming into leaf
and it's almost warm.

I don't remember anything about hydrangeas

or my grandfather's house painted white
and the low blue gate and the parlour all quiet.
How the sound of cars made me cry for my mother
and I don't remember the crash
and the boy stood watching, my mother shouting.
I don't remember crayons
and how the best colour was gold or silver,

or the space beneath the window you could hide
if you didn't mind spiders. I don't remember Widdop
or any fox like a flame, the perfume
and vomit in my sister's room.
How raspberries boiled on the stove.
I don't remember the maggots rising.
I don't recall any deep snow.

If it hurt
and I couldn't stop it, my head underwater,
if I couldn't breathe, then I do not remember.

I don't remember the tape Dawn made me.
or the songs that were on it
or the summer of strikes and rats in the street,
or a bottle of Concorde before we went out.
I don't remember the smell of the flat, the fruit gone off,
the puppet who saw all my sins

and I don't remember the taste of blood
or if I had pethidine or if I threw up
and my hand turned black or if it swelled up.
I don't remember a dying dog
or the policemen lying in court

and the moon from the window in Broadoak.
I don't remember the hopeless sky
or the heat and the plane door opening,

and my tent in the woods or Spain or France,
the word for ants. How my hands got so tired
and my arms so scarred – I don't remember

Anna Karenina and knock-off from Asda's
or the fire outside Debbie's and how drunk we all were.
I don't remember bed with my mother,
I don't remember the prayers or her voice
or how soft her cheek was
when she bent down to kiss me, god help me,
I cannot remember her smell.

Open Door Policy

Maybe one day, you'll walk through a door
inside you. It isn't your home,
but you'll be welcomed and asked to stay.

There are people in there. Like a gift,
they'll receive you
and no one will fear for your health

or your teeth, the state of you.
How you are a cliff about to fall
and everyone near is in danger.

All that you need is a sofa
and maybe the telly on low.
There will be no questions,

only the lines of sun on the curtains.
If you want it, a bed for the night.
They heard you before you arrived

and though you've carried your storm
to their door, here is calm.
You are not high waves

or a ship going down. You won't sink
with your people inside you.
No one will drown.

You don't need to be saved
or mended. Just somebody's hand
on your back,

a coffee with milk, some cake.
You are not the moon
dragging cold tides behind you.

You are not even star
or fire. Someone can warm you.
Someone can touch you.

One day, you'll walk through that door.
You'll rest on that sofa.
You'll stay there forever.

I came back

to the sound of birds in the morning,
to heavy rain falling. Back to the holding of hands.
I came back from the storm
to shelter. Though they said
there was no way back
I came back in a taxi, by darkness
and no one could see my face.

I came back from the brink,
from Broadoak. There was screaming
inside my ears. I came back running,
back from not speaking.
I made the same noise for years.
I came back by grafting, back
with my arms open wide and laughing.

I was brought back by daisies.
I was brought back by doctors.
Saved by a surplus of air
because somebody needed to breathe it;
I came back to the feeling of mud, I forgot
I forgot how to cross the road.

I was not brought back by love.
I was brought back by stone
and by falling. I was brought back
by hitting the floor. I was wrapped in a blanket,
brought back by hurting,
by the sight of my own insides
and I did not like it and I could not stop it
but back is the way I came.

I was brought back by words
though I didn't believe them,
I came back to a yard in the sun.
I was brought back by pain that I could not escape.

When they stitched me, I could not run
I was sweating. I will never forget them.
I came back to my mother's eyes
and the sound of the telly left on.

I came back the long way round
and I did not mind about distance.
I was brought back by violence, my own.
I came back for vodka, I came back for fire,
for your animal breath in my ear.
For the colour of leaves in the darkness.
I came back for your eyes in the darkness;

to houses that did not care.
For tracing the flames with my fingers,
how you parted my knees with your hands
and when the fires had all lost their voices
I came back from the page's blank stare.
I was brought back to words: moon,
falling. I was right I was right all along.

I came back.
I lived through thunder.
And I did not come back for the sun.

The Lost King of Calderdale

Through decades of battle,
from farms sunk to rubble
by weather and trouble,

from homes smashed to pieces
by Corn Laws and taxes,
by flood and fast waters,

through industrial towns packed with
back-to-back houses
and airborne diseases,

the skies full of thunder,
the streets two foot under,
my people were searching for years.

When the floodwaters drained
from the wreck of the valley,
by low-light they found me.

I was clinging alone to a tree.
I was living on dirt and rain.
It was like I had never been clean.

When they touched me,
it caused me great pain.
When they swung me high into the air:

when they shouted my name;
when they gave me my throne:
it was bracken.

And damage.
And stone.
My people

through wind and high waters,
you have carried me home
on your backs for no wages.

I will not forget this.

I sing for the man on the bus

and the sense that he makes of my arms.
I won't sing him songs about horses and fences,
encounters with tigers. I'll sing him the song
that I sang for the woman who screamed in the Spar,
for the history she saw on my skin.

I sing for my skin and what it contains,
for the map of me laid down in lines.

I sing for my brains, and the mains,
for all unspent power; the coal in my cellar.
I sing for my fire, for the dirt on my fingers.
I am boxes, I don't know what's in me,
but I sing through all my closed doors
to the people I hear locked there inside,
to the birds in my chimney, my unspoken heart
and from all of my organs, their unknowing functions,
I sing my unstoppable fact.

For the rivers run dry in the trying;
the songs that I sing when I'm sleeping; I sing for my waking,
for the racket of crows on the slates in the morning.
A song for my stone, for the fossils I find there,
the insects in amber, the stories laid down
in mud in each strata.

For I am a creature, my stomach is motor
and I sing for the lakes I've swum in and drunk from.
For the fish in my gut, belly-up;
the orchards of fruit trees, stripped.
I sing to the ruined hive
and the acres of grass, grazed short.

My arms sing a terrible song
to the kids in the street.
I sing all the names that they call me.
I sing to my skin to forgive me, to
hold me.

74

Flood as Redemption

In knowing the value of light
when it has gone out.
In knowing the true weight of rain:

the carpet will stink
and the fridge will not make it.
In seeing what needs to be done

and in doing it;
wading in up to your waist.
In staring the sky in the face,

in meeting the storm head on
in the drink of it,
in how you were soaked to the skin

in the rain sweeping in;
in how all your rivers were one
in the chemistry of it:

molecules pushed to their limit;
in the moment of pivot
and spill.

In what you thought
would hold forever:
earth gone to water,

trees turned to river;
the shifting of boulder,
the bringing together of neighbour and stranger

in the swim of it.
In what it did
to our town.

In knowing it will come again
and in singing it.
Writing it down.

Teaching Your Daughter to Swim

in open waters
though you don't know the depth
of the lake at its centre; who might have died there,
whether the pike will scare her or bite her,
if the current will pull her down.

At the level of water, the mountains are higher.
The cold is a world she will walk to and enter
where deep mud is softer than skin.
Let the pebbles swim under her feet.
All the darkness beneath her

is answered by birds
and the trees will be tall and kind.
The sun will light up the water above her.
When there's no ground left to stand on,
then she'll fly.

Though the cold makes her teeth ache
she can take it. The rain cannot soak her,
the swan will not harm her. No dead man
will reach out his hand. You will watch her
leaving the shore behind

and the current will flow
the right way. That day,
the water will hold her
and take her far from you.
Now let her go from you. Let go.

Since I woke up as a spider

I'm not scared of heights
any more, or casting myself to the wind.

Through my multiple eyes,
sun is everywhere

and in the morning, there's jewels.
I have a thousand babies

and there's more in this head now
than darkness.

Everything I catch is
mine.

My body is pen –
I write it in lines of light

and there's nothing that can't be broken,
nothing that I cannot mend.

Death is only one step away:
mainly, it comes from the sky

and sky is something like
joy. I am not afraid

of myself. I've a gut full of silk
and legs to spare.

and at last,
I know where I'm going.

I'm at the centre of it.
Nothing can shake me off it.

I woz ere

I was stood at the window. The city was all lit up.
I was elsewhere, taking a train.
I was somewhere where no one could follow. I was legging it.
I was slung in the back of a van. I was in Menorca. I was in bad
   trouble.
Nobody knew where I was. I was in the wrong place.
I was outside, having a fag. I was in Granada, four a.m.
I was in love. I was coming I was coming

I was on the attic stairs and there were ghosts.
I was always too late to bed. I was fucking
a man with a beard. I was walking home from clubs
the birds were singing I was home
there was a shape in the door. It was not my mother.
It was like I was in a dream. I was climbing.
I was looking down. I was being a man.
I was a thought in someone else's head
and I did not know who they were.
I was in a very bad part of town.

I was saying good bye. I was in her arms. There were terrible words
in her mouth. I was in her belly.
I was watching the clock spin back I was going mad. Nobody said
that this was a road I should not have walked.
I was above myself I was watching.
I was in the front seat and she was shouting
where's Clare and I was on her knee
and she was holding me. There was blood on my hands.
I was refusing to say my own name.

I was not there when she died. I was at work
I was working. I was getting drunk
in a field somewhere. I was in Dublin
looking for her bike I would have known it.
I was looking for her name. I was on Facebook I was on Skype.
I was pissing by preference in gutters.

I was watching the first day start. I was in Halifax.
I was eating toast. I was awake on a coach late night.
There were snakes. I was being a father.
I was being a silver birch. Her arms were round me.
I could feel myself crying. Where were you.
I was here.